Inklings Book 2008

Grateful acknowledgment is made to the following young authors for contributing their short stories.

Caleb Adderley
Suah Cheong
Charlotte Rayfield
Serena Starr
Raidy Clare Stronk
Megan White

Printed in the USA
First Printing: December 2008
978-0-578-00302-3

A Society of Young Inklings Publication

Table of Contents

Foreword

Every week, I have the incredible privilege of working with young writers, including the ones featured in this book. I am continually amazed by their creativity, their passion and their determination. The Inklings Book 2008 showcases exceptional stories by writers in 5th-9th grade, as well as their unique perspectives on the art of writing.

Throughout this book, you'll be invited to peek inside the revision process. Revision allows an author to shape their story with specific goals in mind. Perhaps a writer wants to keep you on the edge of your seat, unwilling to put their story down. That writer will likely spend a great deal of time revising the pace of their story, making sure the reader can't help but turn page after page after page. Another writer might want you to see their story as though it were a movie. During revision, this writer will focus on description. How can they describe each moment so the reader can smell, feel, taste, see and hear their story?

As you read, we hope you'll be inspired to write and revise stories of your own. At the Society of Young Inklings our goal is to inspire and encourage young writers, whether they've been writing for a very long time, or are just starting to dream about creating their own stories.

What is an Inkling? We're so glad you asked! Inklings are young writers, 1st grade through high school, who promise to:

- Write about what truly matters to us.

- Expect imperfection from first drafts... We use first drafts as clay from which to form final pieces.

- Play with words, experimenting until our stories are delicious.

- Curiously explore and observe the world because we know stories are in the details.

- Marinate ourselves in superb stories, learning from master storytellers.

- Share our writing with others.

- Write. We do not just think about writing!

- Encourage other Inklings.

- Continually strive to become better writers.

We hope you'll join us! You can learn more about The Society of Young Inklings at www.younginklings.com.

Beginnings and Endings

Though the beginning of the story is the first thing an author writes, it's also often the last thing they revise.

In *Dreams Come True*, Megan White created a bookend effect, in which she tied her first paragraph to the last one. After she finished her story, she revised both the beginning and the end to strengthen the connection between them.

As you read, notice how this bookend effect allows Megan to tie up her loose ends and give her story a strong ending.

Megan White

Megan is 10 years old. Her family includes mom, dad, and brother, with a horse, a dog and a cat. She is in 5th grade, and has a fantastic teacher. She has written a few other books like this one, except not about racehorses.

Here are some of Megan's thoughts on the writing and revision of *Dreams Come True*.

Where did you get the inspiration for your story?

> The inspiration was how much I love horses. They really are fun, and special too.

When you experimented with different beginnings and endings, what did you try?

> I tried a lot, but this was my favorite. Another one I tried was that Sunny saw Rocket run in the Derby, and the end wasn't quite as detailed.

Did you ultimately decide to change your beginning and end to one of the alternates you tried, or did you stick with what you wrote in the first place? Why?

> Actually, I did choose an alternate. This was one I thought up a little later, after the first one I tried out. The reason I chose to switch it was that this one was more detailed and descriptive.

Dreams come True

by Megan White

11

Rocket came back from the Kentucky Derby sweaty and tired. She yelled at me when I tried to ask what it was like.

"SHUT UP ALREADY!" she screamed when I persisted.

She had taken my dream and wouldn't even tell me what it was like. I desperately wanted to race, but against whom? And where? My mother, Rosie, was a Grand Prix jumper. Would I follow her, or Rocket? These questions flew through my head as my owner, Melissa, yanked me to the crossties.

"Come on Sunny, lets go!" she growled as she hooked the clips to my halter.

Melissa dragged the grooming kit out.

"Melissa, don't forget to pick out her hooves!" yelled Mrs. Valores.

Melissa groaned and got the hoof pick out. When we finally got away from the barn, Melissa led me away from the arenas.

Instead, she led me towards the old racetrack. Mrs. Valores trotted Rocket out to us. She smiled at Melissa. As soon as Melissa had gotten me onto the rough soil, I picked up a canter. Melissa pulled back, telling me to stop.

This was confusing, since I'd only seen horses galloping out here before. After a full lap of walking, Melissa asked for a trot. I really wanted to gallop, like Rocket was doing. Mrs. Valores was asking Melissa if she wanted to gallop. I tossed my head up and whinnied, but Melissa shook her head. I ducked my head and did a really little buck, but Melissa just swatted me with her whip. I still was a little mad, but I could handle it if she would let me go fast.

"Melissa, Sunny wants to gallop. If you don't let her, she has plenty of ways to get you out of the way," Melissa's mother scolded as she galloped by with Rocket.

I felt only the touch of Melissa's heels at my sides, and I was gone. I felt like I was flying and didn't even realize that I was whizzing past Rocket. Melissa was jabbing at my bit trying to get me to slow down.

"MOM!" she shrieked, and that brought me back to reality.

I slowly took myself to a walk and let Melissa breathe. Soon, I heard Skye's hoof beats. Skye was my friend and her rider, Sofia, was good friends with Mel. Skye and Sofia trotted up and we started talking. After a while, a huge horsefly buzzed down to us. I whinnied and backed away.

14

"HORSEFLY!" Sofia yelled, and the terrible creature landed on Skye's shoulder. Skye didn't move.

Sofia slowly brought her hand down and smacked it. Skye relaxed and trotted back to me. Sofia asked if Mel wanted to gallop with her. Mel almost shook her head, but considered it a moment and nodded.

"This time I'll stay in control," I silently promised her.

This time, as I'd promised, I stayed at exactly the same pace as Skye. Obviously, Mel relaxed a LOT when she discovered that. She smiled big at Sofia. Sofia grinned back and we went a little faster. We kept speeding up until we were doing a gentle breeze. Mel wanted to walk and at that point, I did too. Then, after three laps of walk, Mel asked Sofia if she was up for a race. I know I was! Sofia said yes very enthusiastically. We started where the faded black and white checkered flag lay on the ground.

"Mom! Can you start us?" Mel asked her mother. Mrs. Valores trotted over.

"One, two three, GO!" she shouted.

I was in front of Skye within the first yard. I felt free again, even though I was being careful to feel for Mel's hands. When she told me to go faster, I was surprised, but happy.

"Mom! We should enter Sunny in a real race!" Mel shouted as we sprinted past the finish.

"Yah!" Sofia screamed, still only ¾ of the way there. I smiled to myself. That would be fabulous!

I stood in the trailer as it rumbled down the lane to the Santa Anita racetrack. I was so excited! When they started putting the tack on, the saddle was so small and light, I could run more easily! When Melissa got on, I was ready. She walked me up to a big wall though! Then she and some men dragged me into a big box. Why wasn't I running?

Mel stroked my neck. Then I heard the noise. Screams and yells and clanks and thumps, oh my gosh, I was so scared! Then the wall flew up. How? Mel kicked me. I saw other horses take off. I felt Mel smack me with the whip. I took off bucking. She didn't like that. Then I galloped away.

Apparently I had already lost. I was mad at myself. It wasn't that different from my race with Skye!

"Melissa, it's okay. It's her first one!" Mrs. Valores said.

I concluded that race with a promise to win the Kentucky Derby.

Four months later, after practicing so much I thought I would break down, the Kentucky Derby came. I was shipped to Kentucky, revved up and read to go. This time, I walked through a door to get to the track.

"I will win this, the Preakness, and the Belmont and get the Triple Crown!" I promised Mel.

She gave me a nervous pat. When we got to the big box again, I tried to stay calm. The wall sprang open. Mel kicked me and I leaped forward.

One of the bigger, stronger horses yelled, "Out of my way, you tiny flea!"

But, he stopped talking and stared when he saw that I was four feet in front of him.

"Hey! Ya'll gotta make way fa me!" shouted a big, long-legged, mean looking horse.

"Why?" I yelled.

He didn't answer. I looked away and focused. Four huge horses were the only obstacles in between me and the finish line. Then, the two horses that had spoken to me darted in front. Mel knew I was trying and didn't kick me. There was only ¼ of a mile until the end of the race.

"Come on, Sunny, you can do it!" a familiar voice called.

Skye! I knew she'd come! I tried harder. I couldn't let Skye down. Before I knew it, everyone was cheering my full name.

"Sunshine, Sunshine, Sunshine, Yah!" came the cheers. I perked my ears at the stands.

"You did it!" Mel said, so happy that she was breathless. Some big, well-dressed men led me to the winners' circle. A skinny woman was talking.

"…And so, I conclude this report with the words, Sunshine Valores has a one in three chance of getting the Triple Crown!"
After that, I heard and felt nothing. I was too excited. My and Mel's dream was one third of the way come true! That night, I told everyone about it. Their moods changed at every sentence. When I told them about the horse with the weird accent, they gasped at how rude he was.

When I told them about the way he cut me off, they shook their heads and said things like, "Rude boys are not going to get a herd," and "Well, payback without anything to pay back! Goodness!"

When I finished, Rocket reminded me that there were still two races to go. I decided to go to sleep then, and woke up to Mel's shrieks.

"SUNNY! MOUNTAIN LION!"

I leaped up suddenly, seeing a huge wildcat ready to pounce on me. I galloped towards the stallion of our herd, Sir Runaway, with the creature at my heels. I got to the rest of the herd, and they huddled around me. Runaway kicked and bit the wildcat, and eventually the creature stalked out to the forest.

Mel ran up to me, and said that she would keep me in a stall now. I looked back at the herd I loved. Mel saw that, and whispered something to Runaway.

The morning of the Preakness was a mess of warm up, tacking up, last minute plans, preparing horses, everything. I felt good, so Mel gave me lots of free time.

About two hours later, I was waiting calmly in the box. The wall lifted, and I was off. I guess I was in the lead the whole time, because nobody was in front of me. This race was an easy win.

That evening, I had a long talk with Skye. She was being sold as a wood carter to a fat, mean man. Mel was trying to buy her first, maybe give her mom's old carthorse, Molly, to the man instead.

18

But I was working hard to be ready for the Belmont. I was running long distances, fast, with Mel on my back. She was happy with how I was running. Three weeks later, after trying so hard in the Kentucky Derby, and winning so easily in the Preakness, the Belmont came. This time there were hardly any horses entered. I hoped that would make it easier.

When we took off, a horse named Big Mean Fighting Machine (or BMFM) shoved me into the rail. Mel screamed, and I felt her leg wedged in between me and the rail. I swung my hindquarters around, hitting BMFM hard. He tried to wheel on me, but I was yards ahead. I won by half a furlong in that last, special race. It took me a long time to figure out, but the Triple Crown was mine!

Mel did end up getting Skye. So now we stay together always, both of us safe and happy. And truly, the Derby and the Triple Crown were my only real races. But Mel and Sofia raced a lot, and many of the riders at the barn were really happy to be able to race a Triple Crowner. Plus, after winning so well, Mel was always cheerful and kind to me.

So that's my story. What's that? It's not good enough? Well too bad, that's it.

The End

Vivid Verbs

Verbs give stories their energy and liveliness. Often authors will search their final drafts for drab verbs to replace with active ones, giving their stories that final sparkle.

In *So Not Evil*, Suah Cheong added to the humor of her already hysterical story by revising to make sure every verb in her story was vivid and full of life.

As you read, notice how each of Suah's verbs add spunk to her story.

Suah Cheong

Suah Cheong is in 6th grade. Her 2nd grade teacher inspired her to write a fantasy story, just by teaching the class a few grammar rules. Since then, she has been writing stories based on her world and surroundings. When Suah isn't writing, she likes to hang out with friends, text, surf the net, and talk on the phone. In July 2008, she moved from California to Texas and still keeps in touch with old friends. Suah is in love with Italian food, and her nick name is sushi, for how much she likes the food.

Here are some of Suah's thoughts on the writing and revision of *So Not Evil*.

How long have you been writing? When did you first decide that you liked writing?

I have to admit, I wasn't born with the precious talent that I now have. However, my second grade teacher was an expert at writing. When she taught us the basics, I let my imagination run wild and created a story that brought magic into my world. I've been writing for five precious school years.

What do you most like to write? Why?

> I like to write anything that involves using creativity and imagination. Doing school reports may seem fun at first, but eventually gets boring at the end. I also have special interest in adventure and friendship stories, probably because I read those genre books.

You changed some of your verbs in a final edit of this story. Do you think changing the verbs made your story stronger? Why or why not?

> In this case, the verbs made my story stronger. Changing eat to gobble or trapped to capture gives you a better description of what is really going on. Changing verbs also gives you a better idea of the main topic.

What one piece of advice would you give to other Inklings about writing?

> I think writing isn't about grammar and spelling. Its about how much creativity you have. Spicing up our outrageous stories with your ideas is better than best. But there are times when you struggle. Take a break, read a book, or talk to a friend for ideas.

So Not Evil

by Suah Cheong

Part One

"**H**elp!" cried Sam, the fellow that proudly managed Lucky Sam's Sandwich Shop. He continued, "A huge monkey is gobbling up my shop!"

Moments before, an oversized gorilla had climbed out of his egg. His name was Big Monkey, perfectly describing his size.

Massive Banana, who had recently picked out a strange egg at Safeway, was shocked.

What a waste of $1.99, he thought to himself.

Big Monkey was now munching his way through the plastic sub on Sam's roof, used to advertise.

"What the hay!" yelped a man standing in the crowd. "I've never seen anything like this!"

In addition to all the drama, several hometown security vans were filling the sandwich shop's parking lot.

The inspector barked, "Take the dumb looking one into the box, using the net, while I put up some caution tape!"

The sergeants bolted out of the vans and thought for a moment. They aimed their giant net at the ape. As soon as that net got around Big Monkey's body, several banana peels were thrown into the scene. Big Monkey turned around to face his "mother." You could tell by the look on that ape's face that he was burning mad at the sergeants for capturing him.

At the last minute, Sam slipped on a banana peel and was rushed to the hospital! Massive Banana wished he spent his money on a pack of gum.

Part Two

GB: My name is Giant Banana and I'm interviewing the world's worst villain, Big Monkey! Big Monkey, tell us how you became so evil.

BM: Well, Giant Banana, it all started out when your cousin, Massive Banana picked out the egg I was in at Safeway. He notes that I was on sale for $1.99. As soon as I climbed out of that crammed egg, I gobbled some of Lucky Sam's Sandwich Shop, though I couldn't get to the last bite because some sergeants trapped me in a net. I managed to escape after three years of planning at the zoo. I was sizzling angry at the sergeants for ruining what was supposed to be my attack. Ever since that tragedy, I've been evil.

GB: Wow, very interesting. So besides that "tragedy" What else have you done?

BM: Hmm… I've hosted tea parties with King Kong, designed lacey outfits, and painted pictures of daisies.

GB: What?! Big Monkey, I thought you were evil.

BM: You don't think I'm evil? Somebody needs a lesson…

Moments Later...

BM: I never even thought about this! I should've munched him up ages ago!

The End

Character Voice

Each person speaks in their own unique way. One quality that makes a story stand out is a cast of characters who each sound distinctive.

After completing *The Story of a Girl Named Violet*, Raidy Clare Stronk read through her dialogue to discover the patterns of speech she'd already created for each of her characters. Then she revised so that each time her characters spoke, they spoke with their own individual voice.

As you read, notice Raidy Clare's dialogue, paying specific attention to how the characters come alive through the specific ways they speak.

Raidy Clare Stronk

In kindergarten, Raidy Clare started making short, 2 page stories in the classroom. At home after playing with her stuffed animals, she would write stories about their adventures. Now she is in the 5th grade and loves writing in the Society of Young Inklings class. Raidy Clare gets inspiration from some of her favorite fantasy books. Raidy Clare also enjoys playing outside, swimming, volleyball and making videos.

Here are some of Raidy Clare's thoughts on the writing and revision of *The Story of a Girl Named Violet.*

Where did you get the inspiration for your story?

I got my inspiration from thinking of some of my favorite names for girls and then I thought of Violet and I guess I just started to type my story from there.

What did you try when you played with your character's speech patterns?

> Well, at first I tried talking out loud, using different voices to see how my characters would talk in my story. Then I would act it out and see how it felt to be my character and talking like that. After that I just typed it up to see what it would be like.

Did you end up changing any dialogue? What worked? What didn't?

> I did end up changing a bit of dialogue. If the new dialogue worked I'd keep it there and move on. If it didn't, I would change it to something that had a lot of detail in it or I would change it into something that was sort of like the one I typed before.

The Story of a Girl Named Violet

by

Raidy Clare Stronk

In the early 1800s there was a girl by the name of Violet. She was a beautiful girl with long brown hair and sparkly brown eyes. She lived in a little cottage in the middle of a forest with her cute cat buttercup.

People in the nearby village thought she should live in the orphanage because her parents died when she was 8 years old, but Violet refused. The forest was her home and the animals were her friends. The pioneers that were coming from the east wouldn't even be her friends because they agreed with the villagers and thought that their children should not play with an orphan.

One day, Violet was picking daisies with her little cat, Buttercup. Suddenly a little pioneer girl came through the bushes and scared little Buttercup. The girl's eyes were green and her hair was dirty blond. She was wearing a green dress that had little white flowers on it and was wearing a green bonnet that matched.

She looked over at Violet and said, "Are you the little cottage girl that lives in this little forest?"

"Um, yes I am, um..."

The little girl interrupted, "Oh, what a cute cat you have. Where did you find her?"

The little girl pet Buttercup in her lap.

"Um, well... um, my parents gave her to me when I was 5..."

"Hey, I'm 5," interrupted the girl again. "Oh, I wish I had a big sister because I only have two big brothers."

"Really," said Violet. "Because I want a little sister and I don't have any siblings at all."

"Oh you must be very, very lonely," said the little girl, her head shaking as if she were saying no. "Well, I better get going, Ma wanted me to go pick some flowers and put them in a bundle."

As the girl gently put Buttercup down and ran off Violet said, "Wait! What's your name?"

And the girl said, "It's LILLY!"

The next morning Violet woke up with a fright. At her door were police and beside the police was a lady wearing a grey dress. She had white hair and green eyes. She also had a pointy nose witch Violet thought was not so pretty. Violet stood at the door in her nightdress and with the cold morning frost stinging her face.

Just then the lady said, "Come girl, pack up your things. You are going to the orphanage."

The lady's hair was slowly coming down from her bun.

"The orphanage? I thought I told you guys that I'm not going!" said Violet feeling like her life was over and done for.

The lady looked at her, her eyes looking like she was serious. Violet knew what she was going to say. She ran to her room to pack up her stuff and say goodbye to the house she loved and lived in for twelve years.

Once Violet packed everything up she waved goodbye to her house and followed the lady and police to the village with her cat Buttercup. Suddenly she saw the same girl that she saw yesterday.

"Lilly!" shouted Violet.

She ran from the group over to Lilly who was carrying a basket full of apples. She dropped the apples and was surprised to see Violet again. But why with policemen and a lady with a pointy nose, wondered Lilly.

"Lilly, please take Buttercup."

"Why?" asked Lilly.

"Because the only place she's really comfortable is here! Take her. Oh… and she loves berries!" said Violet, while being pulled away by an officer.

"I'll take good care of her because you're my only friend!" said Lilly.

I'm her only friend? Violet thought over and over again. I'm her only friend.

Once Violet and the group got to the orphanage, Violet was led into a room that was freezing cold.

The lady turned around and said, "I am Mrs. Crane and this is the orphanage. Now go up stairs and to the right; that is the bedchamber. You'll see other girls there, so make friends."

Then she turned away and vanished through a dark hallway. Violet turned toward the stairs, walked up them, and turned right like the lady said. Once Violet got there she entered a cold room that had cots everywhere and girls sitting on them staring at her. A moment before as Violet was walking through the hallway she could hear girls crying and laughing, but now nobody was saying anything or doing anything.

On the first cot there was a toddler sitting down and holding a crying baby and on the second there were twins that looked like they were hurt. But near the far end near the window there were two cots waiting to be used. Violet walked over to the one on the right, put her suitcase down, lay on her bed, and started to cry.

Why couldn't she still live in her little house with Buttercup? She also made a new friend, Lilly the girl in the green dress.

"Girls" said a voice from the door to the bedchamber "Get dressed and wash up for breakfast. Remember, it is still morning."

"Ohh" said all the girls.

One girl turned to Violet and said, "Here we'd rather not have breakfast."

"Why?" asked Violet.

"Well they just happen to serve us cold porridge."

"Cold!" said Violet, shocked. "Why not hot?"

"Well you see, they don't really care about us here," said the girl as she turned away and started to clean her face with an old dirty rag.

As Violet was walking down the hallway with the other girls to

the dining room she heard a lady's voice at the front door talking to Mrs. Crane. Once Mrs. Crane moved she saw Lilly and Lilly's mother at the door.

That night Violet had a plan of how to get out of the orphanage and back to her cottage. She grabbed her sheets from off her cot and tied them to the curtain. Then she dropped them from the window. After that she started to climb down. It was hard. Once she jumped down on the wet grass she began to run toward the forest. She felt free. As free as a bird flying through the air. Until suddenly she felt a rough hand grasp her shoulder and pull her back. When Violet looked back she could only see a black figure until she could see no more.

Once Violet woke up from her terrible faint she saw Mrs. Crane standing next to a police officer.

"So you tried to escape from the orphanage hm? Say something girl" shouted Mrs. Crane.

Violet said nothing because she was too scared.

"Ok, if you're not going to speak you are not having breakfast"

Then Violet noticed where she was. She was in the bedchamber and all the girls were looking at her with terrified faces.

"Come girls, let's go have our breakfast," said Mrs. Crane.

"See, she is mean," said the girl while putting on her apron and following the other girls down the hall.

The policeman looked at Violet and said, "There's a lot of us around here so don't try to escape."

Then he turned around and followed everyone else. Suddenly Violet heard the doorbell ring at the door of the orphanage. Violet walked over to the hallway and looked through the bars of the railing to the front door. When Mrs. Crane opened the door, Lilly and her mom were there holding a basket full of blankets and apples.

Violet could not really hear what they were saying but then heard the word "adopted" and knew that Lilly's mom was going to adopt someone, but whom? Suddenly Mrs. Crane saw Violet and looked at her for a few seconds then started to talk to Lilly's mom again. This time Violet could hear a little bit but not enough to know who they were going to adopt.

That night as Violet lay in her bed she could hear the crickets singing and the other girls snoring. As she looked out her window she could see the twinkling stars in the beautiful black night sky.

The next morning Violet was awakened by Mrs. Crane early in the morning.

"Wake up, child. Wash up now. Put on your Sunday clothes. Oh, and put on your boots," said Mrs. Crane.

"Why?" asked Violet.

"Don't ask questions. Hurry girl, pack up."

As Violet was tying her bootlace, she heard the doorbell ring. After Violet was finished she went downstairs and followed Mrs. Crane to the room that they first entered when she first arrived at the orphanage. But sitting in one of the big leather chairs was Lilly's mom.

"So, Violet," said Mrs. Crane.

Hey, that was the first time she called me Violet, thought Violet.

"You are being adopted by Mrs. Montoya."

Violet couldn't believe it; if Lilly's mom was adopting her then she was going to be Lilly's big sister!

"Come on sweetie. Let's go home so you can see Lilly!"

As they got into the stagecoach some of the girls from the bedchamber window waved goodbye.

Finally, once Mrs. Montoya and Violet arrived at Lilly's house Lilly ran from the house and hugged Violet.

"You're my big, big, big sister now," said Lilly.

"Yes I am, Lilly," said Violet, while being squeezed by Lilly.

"Oh, Violet," said Lilly. "Come with me."

As Violet followed Lilly she recognized where they were.

"We're here!"

Just then Violet recognized that she was standing in front of the house she had loved and lived in for 12 years. Her little cottage. And in front of the little cottage door was little Buttercup sitting down and looking at Violet.

The End

Pacing

Stories are like music. Each scene has its own tempo. Some scenes are slow and thoughtful. Others are quick and packed with action.

In *Chicken Run*, Serena Starr has created a series of events that move faster and faster until feathers seem to fly off the page! After completing her madcap comedy, Serena revised paying special attention to the length of her sentences. Wherever necessary, she chose to draw out sentences or clip them off, always keeping in mind the pace at which her readers would fly through her story.

As you read, notice how the length of Serena's sentences cause the story to speed up or slow down.

Serena Starr

Serena is a freshman at Menlo Atherton High School. She has always enjoyed writing, but really started to become serious when she joined The Society of Young Inklings. After taking the class several times she was hooked. Over the summer she wrote *Chicken Run* in an Inklings camp. She based the story off her experience pet sitting for a family who owned chickens. Another interest she has is acting. She is currently taking Drama at MA and also ran Cross Country for the first time this year. She is planning on playing Lacrosse in the spring.

Here are some of Serena's thoughts on the writing and revision of *Chicken Run*.

Where did you get the idea for your story?

I got the idea for my story because I was pet sitting for a family who had cats, fish and chickens.

Before you revised, you already had a very funny, quick-paced story. What did you do originally to create humor in your story?

To create humor in my story I over exaggerated my actions, I did make a lot of the mistakes that happen in the story but I made

them worse than they really were. I also had all of the mistakes I made throughout my time pet sitting happen at once.

Did you change anything as you revised for pace?

I did not change that much of my story while editing. I tried to change the parts I found cheesy, and a lot of the ands I used. We had a reader read our last English essays so I tried to use some of the tips they gave me to edit my paper.

Chicken Run

by
Serena Starr

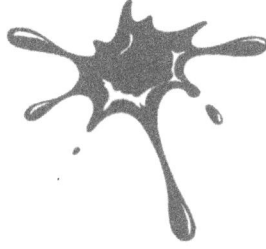

It all stated with a phone call. I was sitting at home doing... well frankly, I have no idea what I was doing.

Anyway, the phone rang and when I picked it up a woman's voice said, "Hello, is Serena Starr there?"

I answered in my most polite voice, "Yes, I am Serena. Can I help you?"

"I was wondering if you would be interested in pet sitting from the 13th of June to the 23rd."

"I would love to," I replied.

Two weeks later, there I was standing in front of the blue front door, key in hand. I unlocked the door and went inside. I poured over the directions.

First on my list were the cats. I walked over to the garage. Oh!

I'd forgotten to mention that the week before I had gone on a tour of the house I was watching. I walked over to the cat bowls and scooped a little bit more than three cups of kitty kibble into the cat's bowls. I then grabbed the larger water container and carried it to the bathroom.

Without thinking, I dumped it into the sink. I glanced down and saw a few pieces of kibble stuck to the little silver piece around the drain. Disgusting!

"Ewwww!" I moaned.

I turned on the water to drain the kibble down the sink, but it didn't work. Determined now, I grabbed some toilet paper and wiped away the waterlogged kibble. I threw away the paper and looked again. There were still kibble remnants in the sink. I turned the water back on and at last the kibble drained away. I took the water container and refilled it, then took it back to the garage.

Cats, check.

I walked downstairs to the fish tank. I grabbed the can of fish food from the counter. A putrid smell was emanating from the jar of food.

As is my habit, I whispered, "a c'est degolasé!" which is French for, "That is disgusting."

Careful to breathe from my mouth and not my nose, I took a pinch of the revolting, slimy fish flakes and dropped them into the bowl. I then quickly replaced the jar and released the breath I realized I had been holding.

"Disgusting," I murmured one more time as I silently vowed never to get fish.

I walked outside and down the steps. Now was my big challenge, feeding the chickens. I took deep calming breaths as I took out the first scoop of feed. I walked up to the gate. The chickens followed. They crowded so close that I was scared to go in.

"Okay, to the other side."

I walked to the wooden hen house and opened the door. The chickens followed.

"Okay, maybe I can get them to follow me here and then I can run back and pour in the food."

Silently, I counted to myself, "One, two, three."

I quickly walked to the opposite gate and into the pen. Inevitably, the chickens followed.

"Okay, chickens. Go get your food."

With that, I dumped it into the bucket. Victory was mine. The chickens pecked at their food, paying no attention to me.

I went back to the feed, grabbed a second cup, and then dumped it into the bucket. I grabbed the water container and stepped out of the pen tapping the door shut with my foot, then walked to the other side of the pen. I set down the bucket and walked inside the hen house, pulling from my pocket a small paper bag for collecting eggs.

My luck was good, for there were four eggs. As I reached for them, a chicken came into the coop. My heart leaped. Chickens were beginning to scare me.

"Shoo!" I said. "Go away, chicken."

I gave the chicken an evil glare, which he returned with a cock-headed, mindless stare.

I grabbed two eggs and put them into the bag. The chicken came closer.

"No! Bad chicken!"

I started reaching for the third egg. The chicken advanced. I stomped, semi-frightening the chicken and in the pause after my stomp, I grabbed the last two eggs and quietly stepped out of the hen house into safety.

I set down the eggs and emptied the two water containers. I walked up the stairs to the hose. I filled the water containers and picked up the big one. There was no way I could carry both down the stairs at once.

"Aha!"

With my mastermind skills, I had devised a plan.

I carried the bottle down a few steps, and then raced back up for the next. I continued my plan of action until I was down the steps. I had no trouble putting the small container back. It was the large one that was my major problem. I stepped in to the barbed wire corral and careful to open and close the gate behind me, flipped the container over onto the rest. In the process, I spilled water all over my shoes. So angry and disgruntled, I headed toward the gate. It was open and a chicken was out.

"Oh no!" I whimpered.

I ran out, shutting the gate behind me. In a strange squatting position, my hands outstretched, I jumped. So did the chicken. I lunged again, this time grabbing him.

"Ah ha!" I said in triumph.

Chicken under one arm, I opened the gate and then shut it just as quickly. The other two chickens were attempting to join their friend on the other side of the fence. I scurried to the other door and opened it. One of the chicken's wings got free. I banged the door a few times to frighten the other chickens and dropped the chicken unceremoniously on the floor. I closed the door.

Shuddering, I wiped my shirt, as if somehow my action would clear the chicken grime. I clambered back up the brick stairs of the back yard, up through the house and through the front door. I stuck the key in the door and locked it behind myself.

Turning around I sighed, "Well at least this job can only get better."

I pushed myself away from the blue wooden door and started off down the hill to my house.

The End

Descriptive Detail

When an author adds details that describe not only their story's sights, but also its sounds, feels, tastes and smells, the reader enters a world that feels almost real.

In *Jeremy the Dog*, Charlotte Rayfield played with how to add descriptive detail without slowing down the action of her plot.

As you read, notice how Charlotte's description brings her story to life.

Charlotte Rayfield

Charlotte Rayfield is in 5th grade. She started writing in Kindergarten and crafted many adventurous stories with her mother as her scribe. Her favorite authors are J.K. Rowling, Cornelia Funke and Roald Dahl, and when she isn't putting pen to paper, Charlotte can often be found with her nose in a good book.

Here are some of Charlotte's thoughts on the writing and revision of *Jeremy the Dog.*

What inspired you to write this story?

I was partly inspired by the dog Harold in Bunicula because he was really smart and the cat Chester, who was also very smart and always getting mad at Harold. Getting my new cat Leo also added to my inspiration.

What was easy for you as you wrote *Jeremy the Dog*? What was more challenging?

      Coming up with the characters and the story line were easy for me as I wrote this story. Trying to brainstorm different problems that could happen to these characters was more challenging.

You were asked to read through and see if you could add sensory detail to your action-packed story. What did you notice as you tried that particular type of revision?

      It made me happy that I was improving my story.

Did you ultimately change anything as you revised? Why or why not?

      I did ultimately change my story with sensory details, because I liked my story better revised. It made my story sound fuller and more advanced.

Jeremy the Dog

by Charlotte Rayfield

Jeremy sat on the rug in the Rix's living room. Jeremy was a German Shepherd with long straight ears that stuck up like prickly needles. Soft brown and black fur covered his body. He was a normal household pet, barking at strange noises, and begging for food off the dinner table. But, one night Sophie and Eva Rix, the kids in the family, invited Jeremy to sit on a chair at the dinner table. When that happened, he knew something was up!

When the whole family was sitting at the dinner table, including Jeremy and Sophie, Eva's father announced, "We are going on a cruise!"

Jeremy was not too happy about this. They're going on a vacation without me, he thought. Mrs. Rix noticed Jeremy's mouth drooping.

Mrs. Rix added, "We're taking Jeremy too!"

Jeremy was so overjoyed that he would be joining them that he kicked up his back legs, knocking the chair over.

Eva giggled as she turned to her father, "Are we taking Leo too?"

"Yes we are," their father answered, while reaching down to pet Leo between his two pointy ears.

On hearing this, Jeremy went from overjoyed to angry. Leo was their cat and Jeremy and Leo despised each other in every way. With orange and white fur, Leo looked exactly like a baby tiger and he had the attitude of a Tasmanian devil. His green eyes glared up at the family from underneath the table. I don't want to go on a cruise with this mangy mutt, Leo thought.

Two days later, the entire Rix family was packed up. Leo was in his cage, being carried by Sophie, and Jeremy was trotting next to her. With the rest of the family, they boarded the ship and took Leo and Jeremy into the back of the ship, because all the pets stayed in the Pet Room. Jeremy and Leo were a little scared because they weren't used to the salty, fishy smell that the ocean gave off.

Leo was let out of his cage and he ended up being with Jeremy and all the other dogs, instead of being with the other cats. The sound in the pet room ranged from deep to high yips and together it sounded like a mad house.

While the family was off swimming, back in the Pet Room, Jeremy was getting really mad.

"They call this a room?" Jeremy barked in a low, angry voice. "This is where all the flea inhabitants, mud covered, garbage smelling rat dogs stay."

As for Leo, he was really scared for two reasons. First, he was

scared of water and he had never been around this much water before. Second, Leo had never been around this many dogs before! Leo thought there must have been a mistake. Where were all the other cats?

I'm busting out of here, Jeremy thought to himself. He'd had a lot of practice with getting out of fenced areas back home, so Jeremy grabbed the latch on the gate and pulled, but nothing happened. All the other dogs were barking and howling at him. Meanwhile, Leo was backed into a corner staring at Jeremy.

"What do you think you are doing?" Leo meowed loudly to Jeremy.

"Saving our hides!" raged Jeremy.

Suddenly, he bit the latch in the right place and the latch fell to the ground with a loud clang. The gate swung open and Jeremy motioned to Leo to follow him. Leo eagerly did what he was told. He was glad to get away from all those dogs.

The two friends ran down a hallway and down a flight of steps. They looked back to see if the dogs were following. The dogs were running and barking after them. Leo and Jeremy charged through another door that led them to the swimming pool.

Before they knew it, they had fallen into the swimming pool and shocked hundreds of people that were playing and lying on their floats! Jeremy and Leo were surprised at how ice cold the water was and how it made them tingle all over. They swam to the side of the pool and pulled themselves out just in time to see the angry pack of dogs bolt through the door and one by one skid into the swimming pool head first.

Jeremy and Leo both laughed like they were old friends. They shook themselves dry and decided to high tail it out of there. They ran across the pool deck as fast as an antelope getting away from a cheetah.

"Now what do we do?" Jeremy asked.

By now the dogs were out of the pool and were extremely angry. They stormed down the steps chasing after Jeremy and Leo. They finally reached them and cornered them.

"I'll take care of this," Leo announced.

"No, I'll take care of it," Jeremy argued back.

But Leo had already started talking to the dogs. "If you're going to mess with us, be prepared to see me attack! It is not pretty! It will be the end of all of you!" roared Leo, with slits for eyes.

The pack of dogs looked at Leo like he was from another planet. They thought he was completely loony. The dogs thought, what can one little, weak, helpless cat do to us, the kings of the ship?

Suddenly, Leo pounced with his claws extended. His ears were flat to his head. His teeth bared. His eyes glowed red with fire. He landed on the head of the Top Dog. The dog was startled and started throwing his head from side to side, trying to throw Leo off. The other dogs ran off as fast as they could. Leo finally let go of the dog's head and landed on his feet. The Top Dog ran away with his tail between his legs. The rest of the dogs followed, whimpering as they went.

Jeremy, who had been staring in awe this whole time remarked, "Whoa! You are a super cat! Come on; let's go back to Sophie and Eva's room. We can write down our adventure and have a snack."

Back at their room, Sophie and Eva decided to let them stay after hearing about the trouble that was caused by the other dogs. They

didn't know it then, but some day Jeremy and Leo's adventure that they wrote about would become a successful book.

The End

Raising the Stakes

Writers make choices to add drama and suspense to their stories. By raising the stakes of a conflict, giving a character more to lose, writers make their stories more dramatic.

In *Becoming Prince Charming*, Caleb Adderley gave Prince Michal plenty to lose- no less than the love of his life, Princess Angela. After completing his story, Caleb revised to add uncertainty to the romance, so that all through the story the reader must sit on their seat's edge, wondering what will happen.

What *will* happen? You'll have to read to find out!

Caleb Adderley

Caleb Adderley, a freshman homeschooler, has delighted in writing for several years. He first started in the model of his older sister. She has discontinued the art, but Caleb's got the bug for good. He writes when he can and tries to make sure he improves each time he sits down at his computer. When not writing, Caleb is very busy with musical theatre.

Here are some of Caleb's thoughts on the writing and revision of *Becoming Prince Charming*.

How did you get the idea for your story?

I came up with the idea for my story, honestly, after watching the movie, *Princess Diaries 2*, though I almost hate to admit to watching a known "chick flick." However, the idea of writing a story from the position of royalty appealed to me, so I wrote *Becoming Prince Charming*. At first, I tried to make it an adventure by adding a conspiring servant, but it didn't work very well, so I settled for the romance setting I used in the end.

You were asked to try to "raise the stakes" or intensify the problem for Michal and Angela. What complication did you add to make their problem more difficult?

> I added the scene where Michal watches Angela and Frederick tango. I thought this would be a good way to throw a little tension into the plot without ruining the innocence of the main characters.

Did you ultimately include the new scene in your story? Why or why not?

> Yes, I did end up including it because I thought it added tension and also deepened the readers view into Michal's mind.

What advice would you give to other Inklings about getting feedback from others on their stories? How can they decide what to include and what to leave out?

> I would say to examine the product of others input and see if it fits properly and smoothly into the story without sticking out like a sore thumb. For example, had Naomi asked me to...say... try adding more supporting figures, and I created a nosy maid that spied on the castle's inhabitants, it would have changed the entire feel of the story. However, if I had added, say, the servant that complements Michal, it would have added nicely to the story. It's good to remember that it's not always the advice itself that is good or bad, but what the writer does with it.

72

Becoming Prince Charming

by Caleb Adderley

There is a time in life every modern young prince looks forward to. The young men refer to it as "the four years," "the four good ones," or something of that nature. What is it? Simply, it is the time when a young prince becomes Prince Charming. Not so simply, it's a period of four years, starting at seventeen and going to twenty-one, when the prince withdraws from society for specialized schooling, workout, and becoming more handsome.

These years are the young royalty's favorite. Why shouldn't they be? It's when all acne, eye problems, and fat or skinniness disappear. How glorious! But what is it all for? Impressions, dear reader! The would-be Prince Charming must someday become King Glorious and must woo his country-folk… and his maiden fair.

My story starts on my seventeenth birthday. At this time in each young king-to-be's life, all the other princes say goodbye, and all the princesses say good riddance. Except, maybe, for that someone special.

"Your highness! Your highness!" My manservant, Phillip, called from the other side of the double doors of my closed bed chamber.

Groaning, I crawled out from under my down comforter and stumbled over to the door.

"Phillip, it is my birthday *and* my last day here! Why don't you let me sleep in?" I asked, holding the door open for him. He was a few years older than I and just as skinny. He hurried in with my pre-chosen birthday outfit.

"Sire, you know I can't do that! Not with all the decorating and packing you have to oversee! I let you sleep in as long as possible, but now it is time to move. Please, go shower, as your day is quite full, and we must hurry!"

I groaned again and ambled into the large, ornate bathroom. A half-hour later, I emerged, fully showered, shaved, combed, brushed, dressed, and what ever else you can think of. Phillip had made my bed and set my room to rights. He made a quick inspection of my appearance before pronouncing, "Good," and swinging open my doors. Instantly, one of the twenty maids on staff hurried in and placed my breakfast plate on a small table. The aromas of my breakfast were almost overwhelming!

I said a quick prayer and sat down. As I eagerly consumed the two cinnamon rolls, seven pieces of bacon, poached egg, and tea (in my opinion, tea is the best substance known to man), Phillip read my schedule for the day. Oh, it all tasted so good!

"As soon as you're finished with that, you're to go out riding with your Aunt Audrey. Then, you'll be checking your bags as well as picking a book to read or some other sort of amusement for the plane ride. After that, you have a farewell appearance downtown, luncheon with your family, and tea with that *Young Man's Weekly* reporter. From four to five, you have to check the decorations in the ballroom and get ready for the party. The guests arrive at five-thirty and are here until eight-thirty. Your plane leaves at nine. Understand?"

I swallowed, nodding. A busy, but routine day in the life of an English prince.

"Good. Now, isn't it about time you left to meet your aunt?"

I took one more swig of my superb tea and then ran out of the room, yelling over my shoulder, "Thanks, Phillip! What would I do without you?"

I dashed out to the stables and mounted my dark, chestnut-brown Morgan horse named Stevenson. I galloped the small distance to the Royal Park in which we would be riding.

There were two reasons why Aunt Audrey is my favorite aunt. The first, she always gave the best presents! Now, don't lose me here, I'm not saying that's the only reason. But seriously, they were top-whole! When I turned ten, she gave me my first real sword. On my thirteenth, she gave me Stevenson, my horse. At fifteen, after my graduation from high school, she took me on a tour of Europe, the Far East, *and the*

States! Two years ago, after I got my driving license, she bought me my first car, a Cooper Sport with the British Flag painted on the top! If they weren't materially great, they had a sentimental message behind them.

The second reason was that Aunt Audrey was my hero. She saved me from being either a spoiled brat, or a crazy busy one. She always had time to give me a hug and a smile.

"Michal! Over here!" I saw her waving from the back of her white mare, Pearl. She wore a bronze-colored riding dress, and a matching hat topped her abundant brown curls. I smiled and urged Stevenson forward.

We rode for an hour, talking, laughing, and having a grand time. After we returned to the stables, she walked with me to a stone bench in the palace garden. She dug in the big bag she always carried around and pulled out a small, book-sized package wrapped in blue and gold paper. It was a picture, masterfully painted, of a prince holding a gleaming shield and flaming sword. Holding onto his arm, a maiden dressed in a flowing pink dress stood protected from a hoard of enemies rushing at them. High above them floated a majestic angel, her hands out in front of her as if in protection of the couple below.

On the back, Aunt Audrey had written, "Someday, there will be a maid that you will do anything for. I only hope I'm there to meet her." I gave her a big hug, thanking her again and again and saying that I would see her that night. Never would I leave Aunt Audrey out of one of my parties, least of all, my big seventeenth.

The rest of the day passed without excitement until the party. It was a big affair with many royal family members from multiple countries.

My best friend Princess Angela (monarch-to-be of a small country nestled between Switzerland and France that was called Cailvain) was there and so was Prince Frederick of Denmark, another good chum. The evening was a pleasant, if a busy one. There were so many people to talk to, princesses to dance with, and friends to farewell. Finally, the crowd began to dwindle until only Angela and Frederick were left.

"Well Michal, the four good ones have come for both of us," Frederick said as I walked him to his limo at the end of the evening. He was flying out that night two, but going to a Denmark palace for his classes, where as I would be going to an English one. Frederick was already smart and handsome by my standards, but I suppose he had to become more so to rule his country.

"I suppose we'll still communicate every now and then?" he asked.

"Of course! I'll pepper you with letters, never fear!"

We said goodbye, and he got in the car and sped away.

"Michal," a girl's voice said behind me. It was Princess Angela. She wore a dazzling light green dress and white gloves, and her recently straightened teeth sparkled in a beautiful smile. Her complexion was smooth and her silky blonde hair was kept up by an ivory hair clip. She looked amazing! And she was about to leave.

Her limo door was open, and she stood ready to get in, but facing me. The look on her face was resignedly sad. I would not be seeing her for at least three months at Christmas, and maybe not even then.

"Look at yourself, Michal. You're eighteen, have your own car, and you're about to become a man... and I won't be there," she said.

I was very close to her. She was leaving for Arlock, a country city in Cailvain the next morning and would return the same time as I would. But that was four years! I stepped closer.

"Angela... just because I'm leaving doesn't mean..."

"Shh, shh! It's alright. I know you'll be back, and so will I, but we'll be adults. I don't assume that things will be the same, but please... don't forget me," she climbed into the car. I held her hand through the window.

"I won't forget, Angela. I promise."

The car left.

"I won't forget," I whispered.

I waved from the window of the luxury jet that took me away. I could no longer see Aunt Audrey, my father, or my mother, all of whom had seen me to the airport, but I waved to them anyway. I waved to my home. I waved to Frederick, even though he was on his way back to Denmark. Most of all, I waved to Angela.

Angela.

"Can I get you anything, your highness?" My security guard, Han, asked.

"No thank you, I'm fine."

The flight would be a short one, no longer than an hour. I was going to a country palace, not the continent. I pulled out Aunt Audrey's

picture. Would I be Angela's Prince Charming?

I read until we arrived at the airport where I was driven to Rose Castle.

"This way, your highness," Han said, leading me inside.

I carried one bag by a strap across my shoulder. The others were brought in by the servants. I met the staff of both my training as well as the house in the first large sitting room on the first floor. There was Mr. Hartland, my battle tactics teacher, Miss Hartland, his wife and my "Etiquette with the Ladies of the Court" teacher, and there was Dan Crickens, an American who would be both my physical trainer and oversee the "handsomeness" department. I also met my new manservant, Timothy.

Mr. Crickens, or Dan, as I was asked to call him, gave me my daily schedule that would start tomorrow and run all the way until my twenty-first birthday.

After that, I was led up to my suite by Timothy, who wished me a final goodnight and happy birthday and then left me. I showered again, brushed, flossed, took off my shirt, and crawled into bed. I was excited. Very excited. I was excited to become all that I could.

For Angela.

Oh, how glorious the next four years were! The first three moved rather slowly, and I went through few physical changes during that time.

However, I did grow a bit taller and my voice dropped quite a bit. Oh, and my teeth did whiten some after Mr. Crickens reduced my daily consumption of my precious tea. Needless to say, that was very hard for me.

Mainly this time was spent on my studies. For three long years, my brain was filled to bursting with conversations techniques, speech-making guidelines, battle tactics, and thoughts of Angela. My last year was, by all means, my favorite. On January 13th, my 21st birthday and somewhat the start of the last year, Mr. Crickens took me aside.

"Alright now, Mike," he said.

Only an American would use such a nickname with a British prince.

"All the other teachers and I agree that you have what it takes to think like a successful prince, and someday, a king. Now, during this final year, I'm gonna make you look like one. It'll be tough, but if you stick to it, it will definitely pay off. Shall we go to it?"

And "go to it" we did. For the next two months, I ran every day, lifted heavy weights, and completed all manner of heavy-duty exercises under the watchful eye of Mr. Crickens. At first, I thought I would die before anything changed, but thanks to Dan's experience, I soon began seeing a difference. It was still difficult, but I tried my best, thinking of Angela, Frederick, as well as my country and family. Slowly, the strain lessened, and I was finally capable of moving onto other physical changes and still maintaining my present strength.

Next came eye surgery to remove the need for any sort of corrective eyewear. It was hard to take the needed time for the resting of

the eyes, but again, Mr. Crickens saw me through. Then, I under went tanning and skin treatments to remove blemishes still left from my adolescent days.

From the very beginning of that year, I had been growing a beard. Not a full beard, mind you, but a short, smart goatee around my chin. Also through the last year, Dan would keep my mind at work by asking me questions that forced me to recall my training from the previous three years of study such as, "If there was a revolt in this part of the country, what steps would you take to prevent it from spreading?" or "If you had to pick a new prime minister, what would be a likely candidate?" This made sure that I forgot little or none of what I needed upon my return.

As the time drew near for me to return to my parents' palace, I began to get very nervous. What if my looks didn't meet my countries expectations? What if I can't figure out what to do should an emergency arise? Worst of all: what if I didn't measure up to Angela's expectations? After all, it had been four long years.

My instructors assured me that there would be no trouble at all, but I was still extremely skeptical. At last the time arrived and I waved goodbye to my former trainers. Dan called after me on final bit of encouragement,

"I look forward to training your and Princess Angela's son."

Blushing awkwardly, I smiled, nodded, and waving, boarded the royal plane. I was to arrive a full day before a party for Angela, Frederick, and I, thrown by my parents as a welcome home and a recognition that our friendships could still stand firm. However, I would first have to face my family's reaction.

The door to the plane opened and I walked after my security guards down the steps and into the palace. The sights, smells, and overall feeling of my childhood home rushed back to me, as though greeting me as a new adult friend of theirs.

Inside, my mother sat, talking with Aunt Audrey. I let my guards stand to one side as I entered. Mother looked up and gasped slightly as I extended my hand and aided them both to rise. This was the first time I had seen either of them in four long years. They were both speechless.

"Mother, Aunt Audrey," I greeted them. Slowly, smiles crossed their faces and I embraced them both.

"My son has returned," Mother said.

*   *   *

That evening, I stood in front of a mirror in my room, straitening my white tie. Carefully, I inspected my appearance. Beneath my bright white tie, I wore a light green dress shirt which was tucked into white pants and covered partially by a matching white jacket. My hair was gelled back, and I wore white shoes. I nodded, content that this outfit would be appropriate for greeting my country.

I nodded once more, this time to signal my new attendants to open the double doors.

"Good luck, your majesty," the younger one said with genuine enthusiasm. Suddenly, he grew serious, realizing how forward he had been. I paused.

"What is your name?" I asked.

"Williams, sir. Kevin Williams."

"And how old are you, Mr. Williams?"

"Not yet eighteen, your majesty."

Seventeen... he was as old as I had been four years previous, before I left for my specialized training.

"Well then, Mr. Williams. Thank you and I hope I shall see more such enthusiasm in the future."

A look of surprise crossed his face. He had probably been thinking that I would scold him harshly for an outburst. I bowed slightly and walked down the hall towards Franz who was waiting for me.

Behind me I heard, "Thank you sir" muttered in slight shock.

Frederick looked amazing in his red and black suit.

He smiled at my approach and said, "Ready to be set upon by a thousand starry-eyed young females?"

I smiled and returned, "Are you?"

He laughed, "I don't think Angela will let them get close to you."

I blushed slightly, protesting, "I'm not so sure...I hadn't seen her for four years until today."

Angela and Frederick had both come earlier in the day to renew our friendship and get ready for the here. I knew I was as much in love with Angela as I had ever been, but I could not tell how she felt about me.

"And what are you two talking about?" A third voice joined the conversation.

Angela strode up to us with beautiful grace learned over the past four years. She wore a sky blue, satin dress with roses of white and other shades of blue decorating the front of it. She also had on white gloves, and her hair was put up in a tight bun in the back of her head. Once again, she looked absolutely ravishing.

"Nothing," both Frederick and I chorused in answer to her question.

"Hm," she replied, not convinced. "Here, let me straighten your crown," she said, motioning me to bend down so she could correct it.

Each of us wore some mark of our royal status. Angela had a delicate tiara made of silver and some type of blue stone. I had a pure silver crown, and Frederick wore a simple circlet of purest gold.

"Are you two ready?" Frederick asked.

I breathed a sigh, suddenly nervous. However, I inhaled deeply and replied, "Yes."

We lined up in front of the door that would lead us in front of our guests, Angela on my left and Frederick on my right. I nodded to one of the doormen who stuck his head out the door and signaled the announcer before preparing to open the doors for us.

"Announcing- Princess Angela of Calivain, Prince Frederick of Denmark, and Prince Michal of England!"

The doors swung open and we stepped forward, smiling in return to the applause that greeted us. As the cheers died down, a call came forth for a speech! I glanced at my friends, but both were urging me to address the crowd. I gulped, drew upon my memory of my speech

making, and stepped forward.

Smiling, I motioned for them to quiet down, "Thank you, thank you."

Silence descended, and I began, "I'm afraid that this is directed toward the English citizens here, but I'm sure my friends will oblige each of their countries with a dazzling speech far better than this one."

"Four years ago, I left you after a party similar to this, celebrating my seventeenth birthday. Ever since then, the thought of you, the people of England, and my friends here, Frederick and Angela, kept me going during strenuous physical trials and extremely boring studies."

This earned several giggles.

I smiled and continued. "I would like to thank you for planting in me the spirit of England which sustained me for four long years!"

They cheered and clapped, smiling. I was exceedingly grateful now, for those first three years of my training that had seemed to drag on for so long. I bowed slightly and stepped back, urging my friends forward. Angela complied with some urging, addressing her fellow Calivainians. Then, Frederick gave a speech for the Denmark citizens before we descended down to greet the guests.

Mingling with the crowd was interesting for me. Now, using the conversation techniques I had learned, there were very few awkward pauses in speaking with my subjects-to-be. I danced only five times, though dancing was one thing I was taught while I was gone. Frederick was really the prince of the dance floor. No pun intended.

Actually, there was one dance that caused me to stop and watch. It was a tango, and Frederick had asked Angela to dance. While I made the famed excuse of getting punch, I avoided the dance but looked intently on over the top of my glass. Frederick swept Angela under his arm and then they swooped into a promenade. His cheek was very close to hers.

Suddenly a deluge of different thoughts rushed through my mind. What if Frederick had kept closer correspondence with Angela over the years? What if they had become closer than Angela and I were? What if she *liked* him better than me?

The thought was just a little bit too much for me. You'll think me foolish and given to rash conclusion, but the possibility had cemented itself so strongly in my imagination, that I had to turn away from the happily dancing couples and refill my glass. Determined to put it behind me, I took a deep sip and thought of other things.

Later that evening, I stepped outside to escape not only the heat of the room, but also the ceaseless flow of people to speak to. There, I found Angela, all by herself, sitting on simple stone bench and gazing into the small river that ran through our grounds. She looked lovely in the moonlight, her blond hair almost white and her face seeming to glow. All thoughts of Frederick were shooed disgracefully out of my mind and I thought only of her.

I approached the bench, clicking my tongue reproachfully and shaking my head. "Her majesty should not be out all alone like this, without a guard. Shame, shame."

She smiled playfully, scooting over so I could sit next to her. I stared into her deep blue eyes as she spoke in a mock-frightened voice.

"Oh, handsome prince! Please remain with me as my guard, but

please tell me, from what do you protect me?"

"Why from the goblins in the shadows, of course! Other evil creatures may also linger near her, and who knows, maybe even an evil prince who would steal you from your Prince Charming." Was that too forward?

Angela raised an eyebrow and asked, "And pray tell me, dost thou know who my Prince Charming is?"

Suddenly I was kneeling. It was as though I knew what I wanted to say, and once I thought of it, I could not stop it from coming out?

"Must my lady ask?" There was a slight pause. I couldn't help myself, "Oh, Angela, will you have me?"

"Oh sir," a tear shimmered across her cheek and her smile widened as she continued, "I would have no other!"

Suddenly, I realized something terrible, "But I have no engagement ring! This was all unplanned."

She laughed at my mortified expression, and she pulled me up, standing with me. She folded my hands together and clasped her flawless ones over them, looking up into my eyes.

"Don't worry! I don't require one. No, my Prince Charming, lend me you arm, and I think we should rejoin our guests! Goodness knows that Frederick can't take care of all of them by himself!"

✳ ✳ ✳

And that, dear reader, marks the end of my narrative, as my

limousine is approaching the cathedral and I must soon depart, and I promised Angela I would not write during our honeymoon. Perhaps I shall have more events in my life as interesting as this one to write about, but all that will have to wait for later. My driver has opened my door, and I mustn't be late, so farewell and thank you for reading!

Prince Michal of England

www.ingramcontent.com/pod-product-compliance
Lightning Source LLC
Chambersburg PA
CBHW031328040426
42443CB00005B/256